The Haywire Heart and Other Musings on Love

poems by

Rachel Anna Neff

Finishing Line Press
Georgetown, Kentucky

The Haywire Heart and Other Musings on Love

Copyright © 2017 by Rachel Anna Neff
ISBN 978-1-63534-381-6 First Edition
All rights reserved under International and Pan-American Copyright Conventions.
No part of this book may be reproduced in any manner whatsoever without written permission from the publisher, except in the case of brief quotations embodied in critical articles and reviews.

ACKNOWLEDGMENTS

"Daphne" and "Atomic Forces" were published in Issue 8 of *Crab Fat Magazine*, May 2016.
"Juliet Killed Herself to Get Away from Romeo" and "One for Regret" were published in Issue 2 of *Persephone's Daughters*, March 2016.
"Phantasms of Love" was published in Volume 8 of Dirty Chai Magazine, Fall 2015.

Publisher: Leah Maines

Editor: Christen Kincaid

Cover Art: Amber N. Parrish

Author Photo: Kelsie Gallagher

Cover Design: Elizabeth Maines McCleavy

Printed in the USA on acid-free paper.
Order online: www.finishinglinepress.com
also available on amazon.com

Author inquiries and mail orders:
Finishing Line Press
P. O. Box 1626
Georgetown, Kentucky 40324
U. S. A.

Table of Contents

Preface 1

Haywire Heart 4

Final Projects 5

Atomic Forces 6

The Last Time I Remember Happiness 9

Daphne 10

Juliet Killed Herself to Get Away from Romeo 11

One for Regret 12

Stirring at 3 a.m. 13

Memory 14

Ten Years Later 15

What It's Like to Watch a War Over Skype

    I. A Life in Lingo 16

    II. War Crimes (Hearsay) 17

    III. Dogs in Iraq 19

    IV. The Questions We Don't Ask 20

Admit One 22

Moving Out 23

Phantasms of Love 24

*To all the domesticated, feral, and wild hearts in my life—
these poems are for you.*

Preface

Poetry has been a part of my writing from my earliest days, particularly poems with form and rhyme. I also have found mythology fascinating. Growing up and identifying as a woman, I have experienced how myths, legends, and folktales (or foundational fictions as Doris Sommer calls them) shape cultural values and inform our belief systems. Because these stories are among the first we hear, they help inform how we see our place in the world. These stories become part of our cultural consciousness in a way that shapes our interpersonal relationships, metaphors, and even how we understand our place within our larger society. Every story produced and shared within a culture builds upon the stories that came before it. Once a story is widely shared, the characters within that story can become archetypal, the story can become metaphorical, and the plot can culturally socialize its readers.

Coupled with my Spanish literature background, I wanted to have this speaker reflect the idea of *testimonio*, or testimony, where one voice can act as a witness to multiple wrongs. Rigobera Menchú detailed atrocities using first person and her biography, *Me llamo Rigoberta Menchú y así me nació la conciencia*, was criticized by some for not being her individual experience. In this vein, the act of witnessing and reporting using "I" makes the testimony more intense. By using first person, the story is a voice that witnesses stories my friends and I have experienced. However, when women use I in poetry, the audience often takes it for experienced truth and not *testimonio* or a Greek chorus. If women witness, their testimony is questioned (think of Jesus appearing to women and those women not being believed) and if she tells a story, it can't really have come from her imagination—it had to come from somewhere ... and other subtle sexist musings.

One way to question or subvert the dominant metaphorical system (particularly when this system excludes or diminishes the existence of others based solely on the basis of their biological sex and socially performed gender) is to take common stories and reimagine them. By using familiar characters and changing the perspective of the narrative, one can break the spell of the hegemony. The act of questioning a common story creates doubt. Where there is doubt, one can challenge the reader's perspective regarding the original story and moral lessons.

What then, is the poet's responsibility in all of this talk of metaphors, myth, fiction, and fable? Who else is a poet but a person who connects to the world on a deep and empathetic level? A poet serves as the chorus for the daily existence from the mundane to the miraculous. The poet has a responsibility to feel and engage with the world in an empathetic way. While poetry is often dissected into anthologies or inspirational mugs, poetry still has the power to impact the reader in ways other forms of media cannot. I was once told, "Everyone should carry a bit of poetry with them at all times." As such, I have carried small phrases around like touchstones. These bits of poetic images, even removed from the context of the original work, echo throughout my life. For instance, even hundreds of years later, the line, "A loaf of bread, a jug of wine, and thou," has weight. These few words, even outside the original poem, now have a deeper significance. That is why poetry, despite its tendency to be fragmented and separated from its original source, is a powerful reminder of how language can rattle about in pieces that, like gold, hold more value even in smaller measurements.

I wanted to critique rape culture, patriarchy, and sexism. These concepts are all part of the continuum where a person is defined by their physical body. I wanted my poems to be about what is woman, but not only woman-as-body, but woman as a scream against the tyranny around her existence. "Daphne" was published weeks before the Stanford rape case became a national story and the rapist's father wrote that it was "a steep price to pay for 20 minutes of action." I found no pleasure in noting the Olympic symbol for victory, the laurel, is a raped woman's body and that the perpetrator was an Olympic hopeful. Again, like I wrote in the poem, "It doesn't matter, didn't matter, what she did." Sadly, a poem written in the summer of 2015 is still true today. That is the bitter reality of existing in a woman's body. Add race and racism and rape culture, patriarchy, sexism go from toxic to deadly and nearly impossible to find justice against.

Haywire Heart

A hummingbird lives inside
my chest, buzzes against ribs,
darts up and down, green-flashing

wings pulsating against the back of my eyes.
Its bobbing makes me feel as though each step
were between dock and boat. The nurse gushes

about how fast and high it flies. I say
the wings must be red because that is all I see.
The doctor wants to take its picture,

peer between my ribs, so we watch the flutters
together in black and white—feathers flapping
across the flickering screen. I wonder

if this is how rats search for cheese, whiskers
quivering, trembling, searching the dim unknown.
Their electric shock shrieks cry out to other inmates,

voices warning as they push against the bars, waiting
and wondering if tiny hummingbirds breathe
inside them. How many ways I can pronounce

its name? In how many languages can I say
slow down? I contemplate if my wayward bird
found the right nectar. Even butterflies die

in glass jars when forgotten. Do I hold a rose
against my chest to lure it out? Pour libations
of honey and sugar water? Would a hand
cupped against my breast make it grow still?

Final Projects

Your grandmother spent the whole day calling us
Maggie and Millie. You begged me to go
along with it, not to point out her sisters
were long dead. We dug through

bins and bags of plastic flotsam and jetsam
for your senior project. I burned my fingers
gluing green Army men atop decoupage faces—

"You are better with the gun," you said
using the same friendship logic
that had me walking headlong into the woods

to clear spider webs. We dreamed aloud
of a shared house with a bay window banquette,
reading and falling asleep together. Painting

your thick nails, I promised to carry
your children. You pointed at what you hated most
—for years I thought you said key scar because of its shape—
that you lived because a little boy didn't.
I said you were my light in the darkness,

the reason any night I could look up
and know in the dark there were still stars.
I wanted to touch every part you hated
and give them new names. *Cygnus, Lyra, Corona Borealis.*

I needed to kiss you somewhere other than the forehead
while we gathered years of garage sale junk.
I sucked on my blisters and bandaged
translucent thoughts to avoid the uncomfortable gap
between old and new skin.

Atomic Forces

In my high school physics class,
I learned about quarks and tau leptons,
how nothing ever really touches—
the world is empty space filled with electric

fields and the electrons around my atoms
repel the electrons circling the atoms of the world.
I wonder if death is like a white spark of lightning,
if all the negative forces pushing me away

and pulling me down in a constant dance
with gravity will converge as a singularity, a black hole
where time passes faster as I reach the moment
when I am without covalent bonds. I am afraid

my life will be inert. I wonder how many oranges
I could slice open, how closely they would match.
Is the orange aware its rind has been split
and its bitter pith lies forgotten on my counter?

I don't want to be made from rib,
let me be made from sun-kissed syrup
dripping down a broken orchard branch.
Let me be equal in the empty space

of oxygen and carbon and hydrogen.
I have forgotten the Spanish word
for tin and I search my memory
for the periodic table's letters

and say Sn. Essay n-ay.
Like a snail's shell or Nautilus,
first there was zero, then one,
then one, then two, then three.

As I think in a borrowed language,
I find another way of being.
How the vowels of *dime* shift
to become dime. How I am obsessed

with the roots of words like varicose veins
in my memory. How some words
are masculine and feminine. If I think
in French my fork is female

and in Spanish male, but I wrap
my tongue around both and taste
the tines in English. I see a fork. Metal.
The only German I know was passed down

like subatomic particles. I say Gesundheit
and my children repeat the elementary
parts of words without the components
or substructures of their father's Portuguese.

Every night before bed, I say
"I don't want to die,
I don't want to have to die."
If there is a God,

why doesn't it look like me?
If there is only one true God,
does that mean others exist?
What does death feel like,

is it like when the lights go out
in a thunder storm, is it a moment
of darkness and not knowing
if there will be light again?

I cut a green apple in half, then in half again,
each division one step closer to *atomos*.
Dipping each section into sodium
and chloride and water, I sob and say

Why do I have to die?
Why do my parents have to die?
Why do I know I'm going to die?
Bones break like hearts.

Then there were five,
then eight, then thirteen.
I feel the ground,
but I am not touching it.

The Last Time I Remember Happiness

> *"Rabbits live close to death and when death comes closer than usual, thinking about survival leaves little room for anything else."*   Watership Down

Coney has been my favorite term for cottontails
because it reminds me of Coney Island,
holding onto spider-webbed clouds of cotton candy,
hopping from one booth to the next, shooting cans,
jumping onto bumper cars. Oh how I leapt and counted

all of the waves, perfect curves crashing onto condom wrappers,
and lollipop sticks. Rushing along the pier, pockets stuffed with
taffy scattering the pigeons by shouting, "Time for dinner, time to
go home."

My therapist tells me to go back to that place, to feel the sand
and the salt. But the thought of that grit reminds me
how I couldn't scrub anything clean enough afterward—
the curve of the wine bottle meeting the stem of the glass

making a moonrise out of uncorked Merlot. Pouring
a whiskey neat to anchor myself to the evening, I decant
these memories long enough for the legs to drip down.

Daphne

> In a cloud of leaves; all that was Daphne bowed
> In the stirring of the wind, the glittering green
> Leaf twined within her hair and she was laurel.
> "Apollo and Daphne" from Ovid's Metamorphosis

Apollo stalked her. He followed her every which way—he swept through the tree line while she took her dog for a walk. The dog turned toward the brush, growled. (The dog didn't make it to the myth because what kind of a hero threatens to kill a woman's dog to get what he wants?) She gripped her keys tighter, wound the leash around her wrist as Apollo emerged. There wasn't any river by where he kicked her dog away. There was a yelp. Did she drop the leash? It doesn't matter, didn't matter, what she did—if she dated him for two years, if she had one cup of coffee with him after work, or if the Apollo who smashed into her like a wave was a complete stranger, she would still hear *If she hadn't wanted this to happen, she shouldn't have been alone. Hasn't she heard of the buddy system? If she was so afraid, why didn't she call the police right away? Did she even yell for help? I didn't see any bruises. I bet she's doing this, I bet she's saying this, for the attention.* Sometimes people scream and sometimes they don't—some freeze like mice or rabbits or feel their breasts become bark, their ears drowning with tears. Maybe there was a whisper or plea of *no* or *stop* or *please*—she'll think of which word she said over and over, she will wish to forget the sensation of the deluge of thrusts she remembers when her own hair brushes against her lips like leaves. Her body was his victory crown. She became rooted, stiff, unmoving—a story used to tell women to plead to be turned into laurels, to shred the intestines of those who swallowed them whole.

Juliet Killed Herself to Get Away from Romeo

He spent the whole first day of our Shakespeare lit class stealing glances, looking away when I turned his direction. We formed study groups—he made sure to sit close enough to me to be in mine. My heart and hymen had been broken two months before by someone else, that someone who was in love with my best friend and was "never in love" with me. Shakespeare class guy (a lawyer advised me not to use his name, not to be too specific with the details, to obfuscate the connection between reality and memory)—Shakespeare class guy told me I was the first girl he ever said "I love you" to. I was nineteen enough to believe "I jerked off thinking about you" equated a romantic gesture. In three weeks, he asked me to prove I loved him too—*tear up the dandelion your ex gave you, why do you have prom pictures with your ex on your dresser, your friends only call you when they need a ride.* When my excuses weren't enough, I became *too busy* to hang out with anyone he didn't like. He wanted me to keep my phone on me at all times *in case something happened to the kittens and I need to get a hold of you.* I believed the intensity of this love meant we were the archetype of romance—his screeching at me that I was a slut because he wasn't my first, his fists punching the ceiling of my car for looking over my left shoulder twice because I thought I recognized the man walking down the street from class, how he changed his life plans to perfectly imitate mine. I ignored his stories from his time in the Navy of dating girls barely above the age of consent, no matter how much closer to thirty he got. I ignored the hackles on my neck when he first came over for dinner. I look back to the moment and scream at the screen *kick him out make him go make him go now say no trust that feeling it's a bad idea make him go make him go*—I ignored the feeling and spent two years trying to understand until the night when I broke up with him for the third (final) time: I slept in my car on campus so someone would at least find my body.

One for Regret

I awoke a magpie, dressed in black and white, blue eyes nestled
inside a cracked oyster shell. I shook off feathers, draped myself
in pearls. Dangling a glint of gold, you promised if I slipped
into fish skin, you would adorn me in jewels and marriage
would end the quarreling. *Shift into someone I could love.*
Broken dishes, punched pillows, unhinged shower doors
because I spoke when silence was the answer, looked
up when down was what you expected, screamed
when you pinned me in your friend's king-sized bed
at a party. No one said anything. No one mourned
the tongue you cut out of my mouth. Twelve languages,
no way to explain why a caress on the back of my neck
reminds me of drowning, how I feel as though I fly
about the room far above the two bodies below
me. *One for sorrow. Two for joy. Three for a girl.*
Four for a boy. Five for silver. Six for gold.
Seven for a secret never to be told.

Stirring at 3 a.m.

I wake and watch the rise and fall
of your chest, as gentle as a ship crossing
calm waters. Observing the wax and wane
of your dreams, I imagine the freckles on your back
are constellations scattered about the night sky.

Ever the faithful sailor of these nocturnal channels,
I memorize the charts of your scars
—the chickenpox indentations shadowed
by the impact crater down the base
of your spine up around your reconstructed scapula—
knowing that even the brightest of stars burn out
or collapse under the weight of their own gravity.

We are finite creatures in an infinite
space of time, yet I contemplate the shadows
dancing an Argentinean tango
more than once across your eyelids
as I wonder if tonight is the last
I can observe the stars while you sleep.

Memory

I taste you like a fishbone-shaped sob, caught
between uvula and larynx. Unable to swallow
nor regurgitate the lump of grief your calcified
promises created, gagging on this stuck sliver
that my fingers grasp at, almost swallowed
every time your aftershave wafts by me
in the grocery store and I search for you.
Instead, I try to rip and spit out
these little spines tearing at my throat.

Ten Years Later

My memories of you are a soft bruise
when I flinch at the sight of a white car.
Yet sometimes love is more than what we lose.

After drunken shoves stained my arms chartreuse
and berry, pinched with invisible scars,
my memories of you are a soft bruise.

One night above the bar, you sang the blues,
strumming my hair like your yellow guitar.
Yes, sometimes love is more than what we lose.

In our loft, I dodged the toes of your shoes
and waltzed around flung dishes. From afar,
my memories of you are a soft bruise.

I wanted to be the person you'd choose.
I burnt up all our photos black as tar.
Please tell me love is more than what we lose.

I searched for words to tell you that *j'accuse*.
For leaving me with a dove-colored star,
my memories of you are a soft bruise.
Oh darling, love is more than what we lose.

What It's Like to Watch a War Over Skype

I. A Life in Lingo
The dial tone is ringing,
your pixelated face pops up.
You talk about your CHU,
which—until I see it written—
I think is called a Chew.
You eat at the D-Fac,
your next PCS will be for captain's
school. The dial tone is ringing
because the call dropped again.
You are going outside the wire,
not the television show. I forget
all the words, their meanings,
wish for subtitles to your life.
The dial tone is ringing.
I've missed your call.
The dial tone is ringing.
It's your mother asking
when the last time we spoke was.
The dial tone is ringing.
Five men are KIA. Killed in action,
not the car brand. Names to be released
once the families are notified.
The dial tone is ringing.
"What time did they die?" I ask her.
She answers and I look at the clock.
The dial tone is ringing,
I count the hours on my clock,
"Iraqi time or Pacific?" I ask her.
The dial tone is silent.
"I think we talked after that happened," I decide.
The dial tone is ringing.
The dial tone is ringing.

The call is connected,
your pixelated face pops up.

II. War Crimes (Hearsay)
The dial tone is ringing,
you tell me about a pregnant Iraqi
girl of 13. You know the soldier
responsible—he's in a Mississippi jail
for the statutory rape of the daughter of the sheriff
during his mid-tour leave. That same solider
is also suspected of statutory rape in Washington.
The dial tone is ringing.
"They don't believe in DNA," you sigh.
The girl's face is swollen from the heat.
"We'd like to nail the son-of-a-bitch
for this rape too," you say. "But no evidence,
no conviction. At least in an American court."
The dial tone is ringing.
The pictures goes fuzzy as a boom interrupts
our call. Lights shake. It's like Hollywood
with your life in the center. The call drops.
The dial tone is ringing.
The dial tone is ringing.
It was a rocket, a missile,
a projectile aimed at the CHU next door.
You laugh.
The dial tone is ringing.
You check the chamber of your M-16
put it to your head and pull the trigger
while we're talking. You don't remember
this conversation. You don't remember
the sound the click made. You don't remember
the nightmares I still have from that laugh,

that click, that fear it's loaded. You make me swear
to never tell the counselor my memory of it.
The dial tone is ringing.
I missed your call. I set up call forwarding.
You tell me the Iraqi police killed a prisoner
that the threat of sending suspects into Iraqi
custody was enough. The first day you saw
the suspect had a broken right arm,
broken right leg, broken jaw. The second day
he had another broken arm and broken leg.
The third day the Iraqi police said
the prisoner tried to escape so they shot
him. You laughed, "With two broken
arms and legs? Like we believed that."
The dial tone is ringing.
The dial tone is ringing.
The suicide bombs go off more frequently,
IEDs are under every overpass
(my friend's husband will come back,
take one way to the store, restaurant,
church, and take another way back,
because the insurgents—guerrillas, freedom
fighters, wrong side of history—would bury
the bombs along the route, hoping to snare
a few victims: it works—her husband's driver
went back the same way, became a spray
of blood and bits of fingers.)
The dial tone is ringing.
"They're going after the doctors now,"
you say. "It's not enough to kill people
in the market; they're setting one off,
then riding in the ambulance and blowing
their S-vest in the hospital. It's not enough
to kill civilians; they take out the doctors,

those who are still here after all these years
of war and bombs. They drain that knowledge—
it takes, what, eight years to train a doctor?
More for a surgeon? Now the ambulance drivers strip
everyone naked on the street. Men, women, children,
doesn't matter. They don't want to be blown up
on the ride over or after the doctors lean over."
The dial tone is ringing.
The dial tone is ringing.

III. Dogs in Iraq
The dial tone is ringing,
your pixelated face pops up.
"I had to shoot a lot of dogs today,"
you confess. You look like a child
who broke something and has tried
to hide it. The dial tone is ringing.
You tell me about Chuck. How Chuck
killed the puppies the Italian soldiers raised.
The dial tone is ringing.
The call is dropped.
One story you tell me for why is Chuck
didn't want the dogs to suffer
when the Italian soldiers left.
"They don't treat dogs there
the way we do here," you try to explain.
"Treat an Iraqi dog nice and it will be loyal
to you and alert you to any Iraqis coming
near because all they do is kick them, beat
them. Starve them. Show kindness to them,
these dogs'll be loyal to you forever."
Another story you tell me for why is Chuck
was mad at the Italians for being messy,

for leaving the area dirty, and he shot
those dogs to teach the Italians a lesson,
that people had to wrench the gun
from Chuck's hands so he wouldn't turn
it on the Italians and Chuck's squad
had to hold off the Italians, so the Italians
wouldn't kill him for killing their dogs.
The dial tone is ringing.
"I had to kill a lot of dogs tonight,"
you say. "They're feral, hungry, not afraid
of us one bit. It's like looking at wolves,
really." The dial tone is ringing.
The dial tone is ringing.

IV. *The Questions We Don't Ask*
The dial tone is ringing,
your pixelated face pops up.
You tell me, "I want to get a dog
when I get back." I wonder
if it's to assuage your guilt.
I know you've shot dogs,
but I don't know, don't ask,
don't want to be told if you killed
a person, a child, a bystander.
I'm curious, but it's not the question
you ask of someone, not even someone
who has seen you naked for years.
The dial tone is ringing.
You tell me every soldiers knows
the right answers to the psych evals
that let you go on mid-tour leave,
on post-deployment leave. "Only soldiers
who want to end their careers answer

with the truth," you say. "It's about the Army looking good, making gestures, looking like they're doing something. It's a big show."
The dial tone is ringing.
The dial tone is ringing.
The dial tone is ringing.

Admit One

When he broke up with me,
I sifted through piles of old bills,
junk mail, joint bank statements.
In a green box beneath the nightstand
lay movie stubs—years of titles, dates,
show times. I sorted each slip of paper—
most words worn or rubbed off—
our first date night movie caught
in the corner, after which we had shared
dinner, sticky fingers, fries.
He picked up the check—his ticket
and receipt fluttered down. He opened his fist
to crumple it. I said, *Wait, I keep them. Souvenirs.*
For a decade of our lives, he handed me his stub too.
I stacked one on top of the other, perfect pairs,
each piece a story I thought to tell our future children
in the lamplight of dusk, our fragments so faded
they could be cellophane, flickering to the floor.

Moving Out
> *"A jug of wine, a loaf of bread—and thou"*
> Quatrain XII, Rubaiyat of Omar Khayyam

Going through each room in this three-bedroom house,
I cut the tape on boxes packed in Georgia, never opened
in Texas. Each cube contains things we thought we'd get
around to using. In the box marked "X-Mas" I paw through

what is yours, mine, ours. I bought you movies, CDs
I thought you'd like—they're still wrapped
in cellophane. I never knew what you wanted.
I examine the caramel-flavored cocoa mix,

the cartoon characters dancing, a crinkled bow slapped
on top—you always did a half-assed job of shopping.
All the embroidered kitchen towels my family mailed us
that year for our new house, your new job, are mine.

The new apartment in a house built in the 1920s—mine.
This mansion— yours, this photo of the dog and Santa—
ours. Two weeks of sorting and twelve boxes are half-full.
The bottle of wine we uncorked soured, the bread turned stale.

Phantasms of Love
    after William Carlos Williams

I pity my neighbors, three curious souls who must think I
unpacked a ghost alongside my belongings. I have
wandered down the hallway, howled into a pillow, eaten
delivery food because the gas still isn't connected. The
bruised beating of my heart is like the summer plums
we gathered—fallen and split. Remember the ones that

we sliced into halves for sugared tarts? I wonder—were
we always tumbling from branches? Did we plunge in
aprons secured with strings tied by wrinkled hands? The
stones in our palms were as dark as fisheyes in the icebox.
We hoped everything would remain unchanged. And

even when we buried the plums' pits, nothing sprouted, which
made us wonder if squirrels had excavated their graves. You
loved the jam, but never scrubbed the pots and dishes. Were
there too many spoons clattering to the tile? We probably
should have finished the jar before parting—we were saving
it for a special occasion—those holidays during the year for

when we both had a Monday off and time to share breakfast.
Our meals had become as silent as a tomb. Please forgive
me for forgetting your last birthday. The date had escaped me—
I had hoped that when we planted seedlings the next week, they
would make you smile, that one day they would grow. Were
your doubts like pips within a wax bloom shrouded by delicious

flesh and fresh juice? Alone at night, these memories boil so
bitter and brief—I roam the kitchen, the half-eaten jam sweet,
sticky. I want the branches outside to burst into blossoms and
take me back to our last vacation in Japan where we were so
happy together, bundled up against the early morning cold.

Rachel Anna Neff, Ph.D., loves language in all its forms. After placing second in the Betty Fukuyama Traditional category in the Washington Poet's Association Contest as a junior in high school, she was hooked on writing poetry.

Her intense curiosity and voracious appetite for books led her continue her studies through the Ph.D. In 2013, Rachel defended her dissertation, "Weird Women, Strange Times: The Representation of Power through Female Gender Portrayals in 19th and 20th century Hispanic Literature," which explores power and family structures, specifically women, as metaphors or allegories for authoritarian governments.

While working as an editor for The University of Texas at El Paso, Rachel pursued her passion for creative writing by enrolling in the university's online MFA program. Her pursuit of this degree was made possible in part thanks in part to a generous staff discount on the credit hours. By taking courses over the summers, Rachel was able to complete her course of study in two years instead of three, finishing in the summer of 2016.

She is an alumna of Washington State University, The University of California at Riverside, and The University of Texas at El Paso.

Rachel is active on Twitter as @celloandbow and shows off her knitting on Instagram under the same handle. Yes, she still plays cello more than 20 years later after starting in fourth grade.

www.ingramcontent.com/pod-product-compliance
Lightning Source LLC
LaVergne TN
LVHW041520070426
835507LV00012B/1709